Wonders of the Sea

Written by Louis Sabin
Illustrated by Bert Dodson

Troll Associates

Library of Congress Cataloging in Publication Data

Sabin, Louis.
  Wonders of the sea.

  Summary: Describes how the plants and animals
interact in the underwater world of the ocean.
    1. Marine biology—Juvenile literature.
[1. Marine ecology.   2. Ecology] I. Dodson, Bert.
II. Title.
QH91.16.S23   574.92   81-3334
ISBN 0-89375-578-8   AACR2
ISBN 0-89375-579-6 (pbk.)

The sea is a strange, beautiful world. It is filled with many living things. There are tiny fish and large fish. There are tiny plants and large plants.

In this underwater world, there are animals with hard shells. Lobsters, clams, and oysters are a few of these. There also are animals with soft skin, such as jellyfish and sponges. There are even animals that look like plants—the sea anemone (uh-*neh*-mah-nee) is one. It looks just like a beautiful flower.

Along with the many kinds of fish that swim in the sea are the shark, the porpoise, the octopus, the stingray, and the whale.

Of all the animals on Earth, the largest one lives in the sea. It is the blue whale. It can grow to be almost 100 feet, or 30 meters, long, and it can weigh as much as 150 tons, or 135 metric tons!

Everybody can see a huge whale. But nobody can see the smallest living things in the sea without a microscope. They are so small that hundreds of thousands of them will fit into a cup of sea water.

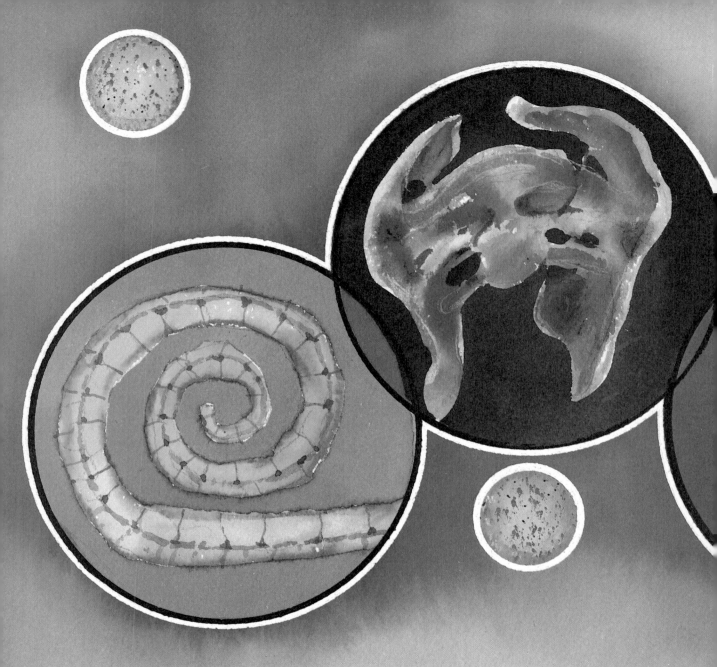

Some of these tiny forms of life are plants. Some of them are animals. All of them—plant or animal—are made up of just one cell. Living things made of only one cell are the simplest forms of life on Earth.

The one-celled plants and animals in the sea are wonderful to look at. They can be seen under a microscope. They are shaped like corkscrews, necklaces of bright beads, stars, and mushrooms. They have many shapes and many colors. Some are red or blue or green or yellow. Some are as clear as glass.

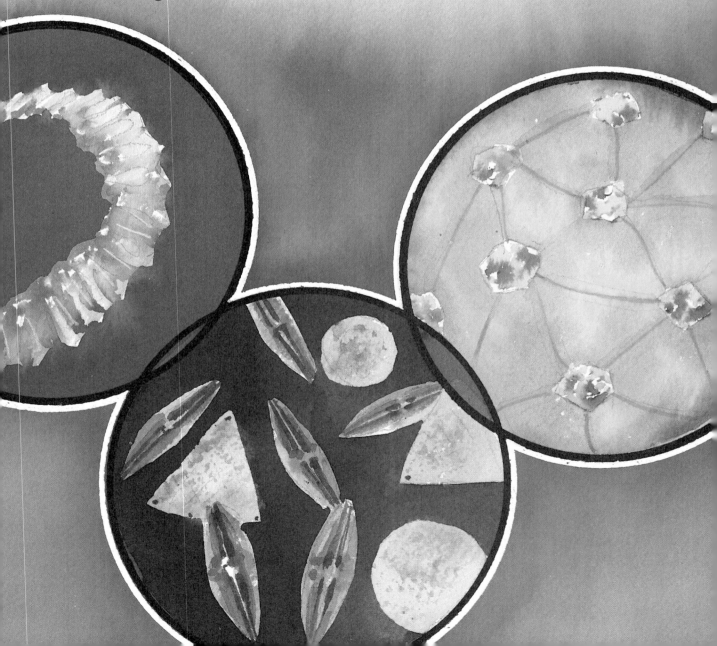

Not all of the plants and animals in the sea are one-celled. Some have many cells. The largest sea plant is the giant kelp. It can grow to be more than 100 feet, or 30 meters, long. Many giant kelp plants growing together look like a forest, waving in the water like tall trees in the wind.

Any ocean plant that is large enough for us to see is called seaweed. Seaweed can be green, brown, or red. Most of the seaweed you find washed onto the beach is green. It grows near the shore, where the water is not very deep. Green seaweed cannot grow in the deeper parts of the ocean, because it needs sunlight to make it grow.

Brown seaweed grows in shallow water and in deeper water. But only red seaweed can grow in very deep water.

Seaweed attaches itself to rocks in the water. At the bottom of each plant is something called a *holdfast*. It keeps the seaweed firmly in place, as if it is glued to the rock. The grip of the holdfast is so strong that even when the rest of the plant breaks off and floats away, the holdfast will stay on the rock. And the plant will grow as well as it did before.

There are thousands of different kinds of seaweed. Sea lettuce is one type of seaweed. It can be found on the coasts of both the Atlantic and Pacific Oceans. Sea lettuce grows to be 3 feet, or about 1 meter, long, and it looks like a big strip of lettuce.

Some seaweeds look very much like land plants. And just like many land plants, seaweed gives shelter to animals. Seaweed protects sea creatures from rough waves, from the hot sun, and from other animals that hunt them.

Living on the seaweed are millions of tiny animals and plants scientists call *plankton*.

Every time plankton are eaten by larger water animals, the plankton are playing a very important part in the life of the sea world. This is because all sea animals are part of something called the *food chain*.

The food chain works this way. Small fish, such as herrings, eat plankton, the first link in the chain.

Then some herrings become food for bigger fish, such as mackerel.

Next, the mackerel may be eaten by bigger fish, such as tuna.

An even bigger fish will eat the tuna. That is how sea creatures live every day of their lives. But without plankton to start the chain of food, there would be very few living things in the sea.

People play a part in the food chain, too. We do not eat plankton, but we do eat lots of fish and seafood. Just think of how much smaller our supply of food would be if the plankton suddenly disappeared!

Sea animals with shells are also part of our food supply. You can see some of them every time you walk along the sand near the ocean. The shells of snails, clams, mussels, and oysters lie scattered along the shore. Seashells come in all kinds of shapes, sizes, and colors. Each one is beautiful in its own way.

Every empty shell on the beach once had a living animal in it. The animal had a soft body, which the shell protected from other animals and from harsh sand and rocks.

Animals are not born with their shells. They must make them. As soon as the animal is born, it starts to eat plankton. In the plankton is a mineral called lime. The animal uses the lime to build its shell.

Some sea animals with shells travel to get their food. They let the water carry them along, as they "walk" on one foot. One-footed animals, like the snail, move along the sandy ocean bottom in search of things to eat.

Other shell-wearers, like the mussel, do not move around much. They attach their foot to a rock and let their meals come to them. They catch plankton as the sea water washes through their open shells.

There are two creatures of the sea that move by shooting out a stream of water. The stream pushes them along, like a jet engine. When an enemy is near, these animals give off an inky cloud to hide them from danger. Can you guess what these creatures are? Yes, they're the octopus and squid.

Octopuses and squid seem to have many feet. But they really have one foot that has grown into many parts. These parts are called *tentacles* (*ten*-tuh-culz). The octopus has eight tentacles, and the squid has ten. The tentacles are like long toes. The octopus and squid use their tentacles to catch small fish to eat.

Most squid and octopuses are small enough to live inside a soda bottle. There *are* giant octopuses and giant squid, but they are gentle creatures that live near the bottom of the sea, far away from land.

The sea is filled with many beautiful animals. One of these is the sea horse. This small creature has a head like a horse, a tail like a monkey, and a thin shell like an insect. Sea horses live in most of the oceans of the world.

A sea horse swims by moving the fin on its back. The little animal seems to be standing straight up as it glides along, hunting for food. But as soon as a sea horse stops swimming, it must hold onto something. So it wraps its tail around a seaweed branch and waits for plankton to come floating along.